The Edinburgh Dinnshenchas

Celtic Literature And Poetry

By

Whitley Stokes

Copyright © 2013 Read Books Ltd.
This book is copyright and may not be
reproduced or copied in any way without
the express permission of the publisher in writing

British Library Cataloguing-in-Publication Data
A catalogue record for this book is available from the
British Library

Folklore

Folklore, or often, simply 'lore' consists of legends, music, oral history, proverbs, popular beliefs, fairytales, stories and customs included in the traditions of a culture, subculture or group. The English antiquarian William Thoms was the first person to introduce the term 'folklore' specifically, in a letter published in the London journal *The Athenaeum* in 1846. He invented this compound word to replace the various other terms used at the time, including 'popular antiquities' or 'popular literature.' In usage, folklore and mythology usually signify the same thing and there are four general areas of study; artefacts, describable and transmissible entity (oral tradition), culture, and behaviour (rituals). These areas do not stand alone however, as often a particular element may fit into more than one of these groupings.

While folklore can contain religious or mythic elements, such as the Icelandic skaldic poetry or the Christian stories of Saint George or Saint Christopher, it equally concerns itself with the sometimes mundane traditions of everyday life. Though many argue this is a successful method of demonstrating societal relationships, in the Jungian view, folklore pertains to unconscious psychological patterns; instincts or archetypes of the mind. These folktales may or may not emerge from a religious tradition, but nevertheless speak to deep psychological issues. The familiar folktale, 'Hansel and Gretel' is an example of this fine line. The manifest purpose of the tale may primarily be one of mundane instruction regarding forest safety or secondarily a cautionary tale about the dangers of famine to large families, but its latent meaning may evoke a strong emotional response. This is largely due to the widely understood themes and motifs such as 'the terrible mother', 'death' and 'atonement with the father.'

The critical interpretation of myths and folklore goes as far back as the tales themselves. For instance, Sallustius (a fourth century Roman writer) divided myths into five categories; theological, physical (or concerning natural laws) animastic (or concerning soul), material and mixed. And although Plato famously condemned poetic myth when discussing the education of the young in the *Republic*, primarily on the grounds that there was a danger that the young and uneducated might take the stories of Gods and heroes literally, nevertheless he constantly refers to myths of all kinds throughout his writings. Interest in folkloric story telling continued well into the Renaissance, and notably during the nineteenth century, folktales and fairy tales were perceived as eroded fragments of earlier mythology (famously by the Brothers Grimm and Elias Lönnrot). Mythological themes are also very often consciously employed in literature, beginning with Homer – and the foundational *Iliad* and the *Odyssey*.

Legends are very closely tied to the history of folklore and mythology, but they are generally narratives of human actions that are *perceived* by both teller and listeners to take place *within* human history and to possess certain qualities that give the tale verisimilitude. Whilst legends will not include happenings outside the realm of 'possibility', they often contain miracles - believable in a specific religious context. The Brothers Grimm, the chief collectors of Germanic folk and fairy tales of the nineteenth century, defined legend as specifically historically grounded, as opposed to their own *Märchen*. Legends and folklore often both serve the purpose of romantic nationalism though; in which a people derive their legitimacy from a common culture, language, race and customs.

The telling of stories appears to be a cultural universal, common to basic and complex societies alike. Even the forms folktales take are similar from culture to culture, and comparative studies of their themes and narratives have been successful in showing these relationships. Although folktales are exceptionally similar to myths, mythology does differ slightly in that it will often refer to 'ideology.' They have most famously been analysed by Roland Barthes (1950s, *Mythologies*), who argued that modern culture explores religious experience in many more ways than we realise. He further posited that because it is not the job of science to define human morality, this is where myths (and to some extent folklore) come in – as pseudo-religious experiences attempting to connect the present with a perceived moral past.

There are many forms of contemporary folklore that are so common that most people do not realize they are folklore, such as **riddles**, children's **rhymes** and ghost stories, rumours (including conspiracy theories), ethnic stereotypes and holiday customs. Although myth was traditionally transmitted through the oral tradition on a small scale, the technology of the film industry has enabled filmmakers to transmit myths to large audiences via film dissemination. The basis of modern storytelling in both cinema and television lies deeply rooted in the mythological tradition. The **Disney Corporation** is notorious among cultural study scholars for 'reinventing' traditional childhood myths. While many films are not as obvious as Disney fairy tales in respect to the employment of myth, the plots of many films are largely based on the rough structure of the myth such as the cautionary tale regarding the abuse of technology, battles between gods, and creation stories are often the subject of major film productions. Folklore, myths and legends are very much a part of our life today, and it is hoped that the current reader is inspired to find out more about this fascinating subject.

THE EDINBURGH DINNSHENCHAS.

AMONG the little-known Gaelic manuscripts preserved in the Advocates' Library, Edinburgh, M. Henri Gaidoz[1] discovered five leaves of a vellum copy of the Dinnshenchas, written (I should say) at the end of the fifteenth century, and now marked XVI Kilbride. For a loan of these leaves I am indebted to the kindness of the Curators and the Librarian, Mr. J. T. Clark. Like all the other copies of this curious collection of topographical legends, XVI Kilbride is imperfect; but, so far as it goes, it agrees closely, both in contents and arrangement, with the Oxford Dinnshenchas published in *Folk-Lore*, vol. iii, pp. 469-515. The articles still remaining in the Edinburgh copy are as follows:

fo. 1a. The Introduction, and part of Cuan O'Lochan's poem, *Temair, Taillti, tír n-oenaig*, etc., both now almost wholly illegible.

   1b 1. End of Cuan O'Lochan's poem — Teamhair — Magh mBreagh.

   1b 2. Laighin, incomplete. Here a leaf is lost.

   2a 1. Nine quatrains of Eochu Eolach's poem on Loch Garman, of which there is a complete copy in the Book of Leinster, p. 196—Fidh nGaible.

   2a 2. Midhe—Ethne.

   2b 1. Brí Léith—Tond Clidhna.

   2b 2. Slíabh Bladma.

   3a 1. Magh Roigne—Tebtha [leg. Tethba]—Loch n-Ainnind.

[1] See the *Revue Celtique*, vi, 113.

The Edinburgh Dinnshenchas.

3ª 2. Berbha—Magh Femhin—Sliabh Mis—Loch Léin.
3ᵇ 1. Sliabh Cua—Luimnech—Sliabh n-Echtga.
3ᵇ 2. Magh n-Aighni [leg. n-Aidhni]—Port Lairgi. Here, probably, three leaves are lost.
4ª 1. The final quatrain of the article Tuagh Inbhir; Bard Maile's poem about Tuagh Inbir, also in the Book of Leinster, pp. 152ᵇ, 153ª,—Beann Bogaine.
4ª 2. Magh Coraind—Loch n-Echach.
4ᵇ 1. Loch n-Eirne—Sliabh Beatha.
4ᵇ 2. Coire mBrecan—Beann Foibhne—Ard Fothaidh —Ard Macha.
5ª 1. Magh Coba—Sliabh Callainn—Sliabh Fuait.
5ª 2. Lia Lindgadain—Magh Mughna.
5ᵇ 1. Findloch Cera—Magh Tailten—Beand Bairchi— —Tráigh Tuirbhe—Lusmagh.
5ᵇ 2. Beand Codhail—Tlachtga—Inbher Cichmaini.

It will be seen that the Oxford Dinnshenchas does not contain the last twenty-two of these articles, and the primary object of this paper is to print the twenty-two faithfully, with literal translations and such notes as seem likely to elucidate what often, in spite of all my efforts, remains obscure. I have added, by way of supplement, three other articles found in Egerton 1781, a vellum in the British Museum, and hitherto, so far as I know, unpublished. The articles now printed are numbered consecutively, in continuation of the fifty-two already published in this Journal. Those most likely to interest folklorists are Nos. 55, 61, 64, 67, 69, 70, 73. In the notes, " BB." means the Book of Ballymote; "H." the Dublin vellum H. 3. 3; "Lec." the Book of Lecan; "LL." the Book of Leinster; and "R." the Irish MS. at Rennes.

W. S.

The Edinburgh Dinnshenchas.

THE EDINBURGH DINNSHENCHAS.
(Kilbride XVI, fo. 4ᵃ 1.)

[53. BENN BOGUINE.]—Beand Bogaine, cid día ta?
Beand Bogaine .i. bo di bhuaib Flidaisi mna Oi*l*illa Find adrullai ind, [f. 4 2] ꝛ fiadhaigheastar ann sil na bo sin go rugastar da læg .i. lægh fireand ꝛ lægh boineand, go silastar ꝛ go fiadhaigsedar[1] annsin a sil go nach feta ni doib. in tarbh robai aco intan rogeisead dothigdis buar Er*enn* fua ꝛ noreithdís go maidheadh a c*r*idhe. Robi Findchad m*a*c Neill f*or* altrom la hinghin n-Uatha. Luid in bo bai 'na beolo sein fo gheim in tairb isin sliab. Luidh mac Neill ina deghaidh[2] a buair, ꝛ gonais a buair ꝛ gonais go slegaib na bu, c*on*aca imbí in martghail sin, c*on*-eber*t* "is boghuine so", ol se, diamba[3] Beand Boghuine go so.

> Beand Boghuine is de dotha
> rocualadar fir is mna,
> don martgail[s]e, go lin ngal,
> rognídh go fir la Findchad.

Benn Boguine, whence is it?
Benn Boguine, to wit, thither escaped a cow of the kine of Flidais, wife of Ailil the Fair, and the offspring of that cow became wild. And the cow brought forth two calves, a male calf and a female calf, and her offspring went wild therein so that nought could be done with them. When the bull they had would bellow (all) the cattle of Ireland would go to him, and run so that their hearts were broken.

Finnchad, son of Niall, was in fosterage with Anè, daughter of Uath. The cow that was feeding him went at the roar of the bull to the mountain. Niall's son (at his foster-mother's command) followed the cattle and killed the kine with spears. And when he saw that ox-slaughter, he said: "This a killing of kine," quoth he. Whence *Benn Boghuine*, "Peak of Kine-killing," hitherto.

> Benn Boguine, hence it is,
> Men and women have heard,
> From this ox-slaughter, with a number of fights,
> Which was wrought truly by Finnchad.

Also in LL. 165 a 45, and, more fully, in BB. 397 a; H. 55 b; and L. 504 b. *Benn Boguine* has not, so far as I know, been identified. A man's name *Bogaine* occurs, LU. 70 b 14.
As to Flidais, see LL. 247 a 33—248 a 11.

[54. MAG CORAINN.]—Mag Coraind, cid dia ta? Ni *ansa*.
Corand cruitire sidhe do Dianche[ch]d, mac in Dag[hd]ai, go roghart sein asa croit Cælcheis do mhuccaibh Dreibrinde. Roraith

---
[1] MS. fiagaigsedar.   [2] MS. deghaigh.   [3] MS. ciamba.

fothuaidh[1] a niurt a chnamh, roraith a niurt retha læchradh Ollnegm*acht* ⁊ a chuanart 'na deghaidh, go rige Ceis Coraind. Un*de* Ceis [Coraind] ⁊ Mag Coraing. Vn*de* poeta cecinit:

> Corand cruitire creachach,
> m*a*c in Dagh[d]a dianbhreathach.
> ba guirt f*r*i feis díanim sluind[2]
> t*r*iana chruit go ceis Coraind.

Magh Coraind, whence is it?
Not hard (to say). Corann, he was harper to the Dagda's son, Dianchécht, and out of his harp he summoned Caelcheis, one of the swine of Drebrenn. Northwards it ran with (all) the strength of its limbs. After it ran the champions of Connaught with (all) their strength of running, their hounds following them as far as Céis Coraind. Whence Céis Coraind and Magh Coraind. Whence (also) a poet sang:

> Corand, a plundering harper,
> The swift-judging son of Diancecht,
> . . . .
> Through his harp to Céis Corann.

Also in LL. 165 a 35; BB. 389 a 17; H. 47 a; Lec. 494 b; R. 114 b 2; Versified, LL. 212 a 14. See, too, *Silva Gadelica*, ii, 536.

Céis Coraind is a hill in the barony of Corran, county of Sligo. *Magh Coraind* is, I suppose, the plain from which it rises.

Dian-chécht was the leech, and the Dagdae was the king, of the Tuatha Dé Danann, who gave Corand a grant of land for his excellent harping (*Tucsat Tuath De . . . . ferand diles ar degsheinm*, LL. 212 a 16).

As to the swine of Drebrenn, see *Folk-Lore*, iii, 495.

[55. LOCH N-ECHACH.]—Loch n-Eachach, canas rohainmnigheadh?

Ri[b] m*a*c Maireada ⁊ Echo m*a*c M*ai*readha dolodar anneas a hIrluachair andis for imirce ⁊ rodeagails*et* andis og Beluch da Liag. Luidh indalanai siar . 1. Eocho f*or* Breogha go rogabh for Brugh[3] M*ei*c in Og. Doluid sein chucu ir-richt brughad, ⁊ a gerran ina laimh, ⁊ dlomais doib *con*a bedis isin Brugh.[3] Atb*er*tadar *ir*is nad bai acu cumang do imachur in ealma ellaig bai oga gen chaipliu. "Cuiridhsi," ol se, "lan in maighe i taid do eiribh *con*a n-irsibh ar in gearran sa ⁊ beraidh libh go maigin i laigfe foa." Dochodar as iarumh go rangadar Liathmuine. Laighid leo an gerran i suidhiu ⁊ dobe*ir* a mun ann, *co* nde*r*na tobar dhe, go tanic thairsiu, *con*id e Loch nEachach .1. Eochu in rí ⁊ fual a eich roleath ann.

Doluid im*morro* Rib féin timcheall síar gor' gabh i maigh Fhind:

---

[1] MS. fothuaigh. [2] This line is corrupt. In LL. 165ª it is: rogart in muicc fri séis slaind. [3] MS. brudh.

The Edinburgh Dinnshenchas.

ba head on Tir Cluichi Midhir ʒ Ma*i*c in Og. Luid[1] fon indas cetna Midhir ʒ [fo. 4ᵇ 1] cucu ʒ capall cengalta lais, gon rallsat a c*r*od fair, gonos-rug leo gorigi Mag nDairbthean fo*r*sa ta in loch. Laighid in gerran ann ʒ dob*eir* a mhun gor'bo tip*r*at, gor' muidh tairsib. Ribh ainm in ríg. bait*er* in Ríb. Un*de* Loch Rí[bh] ʒ Loch nEchach no*m*inata sunt.

> Baidhis Æng*us* Eocho uais
> tre fhual a eich go n-athluais,
> doluidh Midhir, b*r*igh ro*n*-lean,
> gor' baidh Rib i Maigh Dairbthenn.

Loch n-Echach, whence was it named?

Ríbh, son of Mairid, and Eocho, son of Mairid, the twain went from the south out of Irluachair on a flitting, and separated at Belach dá Liacc, "the Pass of the two Flagstones". One of the twain, even Eocho, went westward on Bregia and set up on the Plain of Mac ind Oc. He (the Mac ind Oc) went to them in the shape of a land-holder, with his nag in his hand, and told them that they should not bide on the Plain. They said to him that they had no power to carry their load of goods (?) without pack-horses. "Put," says he, "the full of the plain wherein ye stand into bundles with their straps upon this nag, and he will carry them with you to the place where he will lie down thereunder." So they went thence till they reached Liathmuine. Therein the nag lies down beside them, and there he stales, and made of his urine a well which came over them. So *that* is Loch n-Echach, to wit, Eochu the king and his horse's water, which there spread out.

Howbeit Ríbh himself went around westward and set up on Magh Find: now that was the Playing-ground of Midir and of Mac ind Oc. In the same way Midir went to them, having a haltered horse with him, and they put their wealth upon the horse, and he carried it off with them as far as Magh Dairbthenn, whereon the lake now lies. There the nag lies down and passes his urine until it became a well, which broke over them. Ríbh is the king's name. Ríbh is drowned.

Whence Loch Ríbh and Loch nEchach were (so) called.

> Oengus drowned haughty Echo
> By means of his steed's urine, with great speed:
> Midir went—force followed him—
> And drowned Ríbh on Magh Dairbthenn.

Also in BB. 390 a 31; H. 49 a; and Lec. 496 a, where the story is more fully told. Printed, without a translation, in *Silva Gadelica*, ii, 484, 532. See also *Aided Echach maic Maireda*, LL. 39 a—39 b, edited by Crowe in 1870, from which it appears that the "flitting" was an elopement with Eochaid's stepmother Ebliu.

Irluachair, in the south-east of the county of Kerry.

---

[1] MS. Luig.

The Edinburgh Dinnshenchas.

Belach dá Liacc. Not identified. *Breg-mag*, a plain in East Meath.
Brug (or *Mag*) *Maic ind Oc*, the plain through which the Boyne runs.
Liathmuine, "grey brake," somewhere in Ulster.
Loch n-Echach, now Lough Neagh, between the counties of Antrim, Londonderry, Down, Armagh, and Tyrone.
Oengus, also called *Mac ind Oc*, son of the Dagda. See *Folk-Lore*, iii, 479.
Midir of Brí Leith. See *Folk-Lore*, iii, 493.

[56. LOCH N-ÉRNE.]—Loch nÉirne, cid dia ta?
Eirne ingen Buirg Buireadhaigh me*i*c Manchin, banchoimhedaid do chir comraraib Meadbha C*r*uachan, ⁊ bantaiseach ingenraidhe fe*r* Ollnegm*ach*t. Intan iarumh doluidh Olca ái a huaimh Cruachan do chomrag f*r*i Amhairghin Iarghiundach rochroith a ulcha ann[1] doibh [⁊ roben a déta,] go ndeachadar fo*r* dasacht m*a*crada ⁊ ingenradha in tiri, go nd*er*nadh a n-aidhead ann ar a omhon. Da reith da*no* Eirne co*n*a hingenraidh go Loch nEirne, go ros-baidh in loch. Is desin ata Loch nEirne.

        Eirne go n-uaill, comoll nglain,
        inghean Buirg buain Buireadhaich,
        si rotheich, ni gnim n-uabhair,
        fo loch Érne ar imuamain.[2]

Nó ba ferann do Ernaib fe*ch*t n-aile go rob*r*is Fiacho Lab*r*ainne mac Senbotha me*i*c Tighernmais cath forro goros-dílgend,[3] co*n*idh iarsin do mebhaidh in loch fo tir nEr*enn*. Un*de est* Loch nEirne, *et* quod ue*r*ius *est*.

Lough Erne, whence is it?
Erne, daughter of Borg the Bellowing, son of Manchín, was the keeperess of Medb of Cruachu's comb-caskets, and leader of the maidens of the men of Connaught. Now when Olca Ai went out of the cave of Cruachu to contend against Amargen the Black-haired, he shook his beard at them and gnashed his teeth, so that the boys and girls of the country went mad, and their tragical death was caused by dread of him. Then Erne with her maidens ran to Lough Erne, and the lough drowned them. Thence is (the name) *Loch n-Érne*.

        Erne with pride, a pure union,
        Daughter of good Borg the Bellowing,
        She fled—no deed to boast of—
        Under Lough Erne for exceeding fear.

Or it [the bed of Lough Erne] was once the territory of the Ernai, until Fiacha Labrainne, son of Senboth, son of Tigernmas, routed them in battle and destroyed them; and thereafter the

---

[1] MS. rochraith a chulcan*n*.   [2] In the MS. this quatrain is at the end of the article.   [3] MS. -dligeandh.

lake burst throughout the land of Erin.   Whence is *Loch nÉrne*, and this is truer.

> The first paragraph is also in BB. 391 a 18 ; H. 49 b ; and Lec. 498 a.
> *Loch nÉrne*, now Lough Erne, in the county of Fermanagh.
> *Medb* of Cruachu, the famous queen of Connaught.
> *Amargen*, father of Conall Cernach.

[57. SLÍAB BETHA.]—Slíabh Beatha, cidh día ta?
Bith mac Nai me*i*c Lamhiach ⁊ Cessair ingen Betha ⁊ Ladru a luamh ⁊ Findtan mac Bochra a maccæm dolodar f*or* teicheadh cethrachad laithi ria ndilind fodeigh doruimenadar na badh do airimh in betha in t-innserad iartharach don bith o muir Thorrian[1] siar, ⁊ asb*er*t Næ m*a*c Lamhiach nis-leicfeadh son i n-airc. Dolodar a ceathair ar imgabhail na dilend sin go torachtadar Erinn ⁊ ros-baidh in dili am*ai*l dos-tarraidh in gach aird .i. Bith i Slíabh Betha, Ladru i nArd Ladrann, Cessair i Cuil Cessra, Finntan i F*er*t Findtain os Tul Tuinde. Robi blia*dan* lan i mbadhud *con*id iarum ron-athnai arisi, ⁊ in barc i tudchadar[2] isi go mb*r*ui in lear imon carraig ig Dun Barc iarna dusgudh a huis*ci* dia cind blia*dne*. Un*de* Sli-[fo. 4ᵇ 2]-ab Beatha.

> Rofhuair Bit[h] bas f*or*sin t[s]leib
> m*a*c Lamhíach luchair lainfeil,
> rombáidh[3] in dili dedla
> ua Malalei*n* mor echta.

Sliab Betha, whence is it?
Bith, son of Noah, son of Lamech, and Cessair, Bith's daughter, and Ladru his pilot, and Finntan, son of Bochra, his boy, went in flight, forty days before the Deluge, because they thought that the western islands of the world, from the Tyrrhene sea westward, would not be counted as belonging to the world, and Noah, son of Lamech, had said that he would not let them into the ark. To avoid that flood the four fared on till they reached Erin, and the Flood drowned them as it overtook them at each point, to wit, Bith on Sliab Betha, Ladru on Ard Ladrann, Cessair in Cúil Cessra, and Finntan in Fert Finntain over Tul Tuinne. (Each) was for a whole year beneath the waves,[4] and then (the sea) gave them up again ; but as to the ship wherein they had arrived the sea dashed it on a rock at Dún Barc on the last day of the year after it had been raised out of the water.   Whence is *Sliab Betha*.

> Bith found death on the mountain.
> (Bith), son [leg. grandson?] of Lamech the bright, fully-hospitable,

---

[1] MS. thorriam.   [2] MS. tudchaidhar.   [3] MS. rombaigh.
[4] Literally, "in drowning."

The Edinburgh Dinnshenchas.

The bold Flood drowned him,
The grandson of great-deeded Methusalem.

<small>The corresponding story in BB. 397 b 18; H. 56 b; and Lec. 505 a, is much briefer. Keating (p. 107 of O'Mahony's version) gives a tale more nearly resembling ours. See also BB. 22 b, and the *Four Masters*, A.M. 2242.

Sliab Betha, "Bith's Mountain," now Slieve Beagh, a mountain on the confines of Fermanagh and Monaghan.

Ard Ladrann, somewhere on the sea-coast of the co. Wexford.

Cúil Cessra, "Cessair's Recess," said to be Coolcasragh, near Knockmea, in the co. of Clare. In BB. 22 b 15, we have *Ceassair o ta Carn Cuili Ceasrac i Connachtaibh*; but see O'Donovan's note *h*, *Four Masters*, A.M. 2242.

Fert Finntain, "Finntan's Grave," in the territory of Lough Derg.

Dún Barc, also *Dún na mbarc*, now Dunamark, in the barony of Bantry and county of Cork.</small>

[58. COIRE MBRECCÁIN.]—Coire mBrecan, can as rohainmn-ig*ed*?

Brecan m*a*c Partholoin dochuaidh ar uaill ⁊ ingaire go tríu*n* sloig Ere*nn* umi fo chum*c*ha inbeatha *for* dim*us*. Is eadh leath rola, forsin fairrgi mbaileadhaigh fothuaidh,[1] gorige in sæbchoiri, ⁊ go robaidhead ann, *con*id de ata C*oire* mBrecain.

> Mac Parrtholoin, gnim gen gloir,
> rofhúair samthoghail[2] sirbroin.
> Brecan na læchraidhe ille
> ron-sluig sæbhchoire suighthe.[3]

Nó gomad B*r*ecan m*a*c Maine me*ic* Neill robaidhedh ann. Is e a asna adra*cht* fo churach Coluim chilli dia ndebe*rt*: "Is condalbh sin, a shen-Brecain," et quod est uerius.

Coire mBreccáin, whence was it named?

Breccan, son of Partholan, went, for pride and impiety (?), with a third of the host of Erin around him, throughout the world's straits. This is the direction in which he went, northwards over the furious sea, as far as the whirlpool (so called), and there he was drowned. So thence is the name *Coire mBreccáin*, "Breccán's Caldron."

> Partholan's son, deed without glory,
> Found a very mournful destruction.
> Breccán of the heroes hither,
> A whirlpool sucking down swallowed him.

Or it may be that Breccán, son of Maine, son of Niall (of the Nine Hostages), was drowned therein. It is his rib that rose up under Colomb cille's boat, when the saint said: "That is friendly, thou old Breccán," and this is truer.

<small>Similar tales are in BB. 398 a, and Lec. 505 b. They are translated in Reeves' *Vita Columbae*, pp. 262, 263. See also Cormac's Glossary, s. v. *Coire Brecain*.

The *Coire mBreccain* here mentioned is, according to Reeves, the dangerous sea</small>

---

[1] MS. fothuaigh.   [2] MS. samhthodhail.   [3] In the MS. this quatrain is at the end of the article.

The Edinburgh Dinnshenchas.

between Rathlin Island and the north coast of Ireland, and not the strait between Scarba and Jura, which is now called Corryvreckan, *Vita Columbae*, pp. 29, 121.
As to Partholan, see LL. 127 a, and O'Mahony's *Keating*, pp. 83, 114-116.

[59. BENN FOIBNI.]—Beann Foibhne, can as rohainmnigheadh? Ni *ansa*.

Foibne feinnidh, is e rombuail Illand mac Erclaim[1] me*i*c Doithre f*or* lar Temrach os gualaind Eachach Ailtleathain me*i*c Ailella Caisfhiaclaich. Luidh iarum fothuaidh[2] arfud Breag. Roslac Feargna Fear Ga[i] Leatha[i]n ina dhiaidh, ⁊ immusracht[3] remhi as gach beinn in-aroile go riacht in beind ud, *co*nidh ann sin rodoimeart. Un*de* Bean Foibhne.

> Foibhne feinnidh, fuachdha in fear,
> luidh o Themhraigh i tír mBreagh.
> i cinaidh Illaind na n-ead
> rombi Fearghna, ba f*r*ithbhed.

Benn Foibni, whence was it named?
Not hard (to say). Foibne the champion, 'tis he who struck Illann, son of Erclam, son of Doithre (the king of Sliab Moduirn), in the midst of Tara, above the shoulder of Eochaid of the Broad Joints, son of Ailill of the Twisted Teeth. Then he went northward throughout Bregia. Fergna Fer Gái Leathain, "the Man of the Broad Spear," hurled himself after him, and drove Foibne before him from one peak to another, till he reached that peak, and there Fergna killed him. Whence *Benn Foibni*, "Foibne's Peak."

> Foibne the champion, surly was the man,
> Went from Tara into the land of Bregia.
> In revenge for Illann of the jealousies
> Fergna slew him—'twas a counter-hurt.

Also in BB. 399 a; H. 57 b; Lec. 506 b.
Benn Foibni has not been identified.
Foibne is described in the other MSS. as Eochaid Altlethan's cupbearer (*deogbaire*).
Eochaid Altlethan, said to have been over-king of Ireland from A.M. 4788 to A.M. 4804, as was his father, Ailill Casfhiaclach, from A.M. 4758 to A.M. 4782.

[60. ARD FOTHAID.]—Ard Fothaidh,[4] cid dia ta? Ni *ansa*.
Fothadh gonatuil ann go ceand naí mís f*r*i foghur circi Boirci dia mbai f*or* a e*ch*tra. Un*de* Ard Fothaid.

---

[1] MS. is e rombai il laim lam. [2] MS. fothuaigh. [3] MS. imriacht, but BB. has *imusracht*, and H. has *musracht*. [4] MS. fothaigh.

The Edinburgh Dinnshenchas.

> Fothad Airg[th]each, glan a gluais,
> ro thuil ann *con*a athluais,
> f*ri* re nai mis, monor ngle,
> f*ri* fogor circi Boirche.

Ard Fothaid, whence is it?
Not hard (to say). Fothad slept there till the end of nine months at the sound of Boirche's hen, when he was on his adventure. Whence is *Ard Fothaid*, " Fothad's Height."

> Fothad Airgthech, clear his movement,
> Slept there with his great speed.
> For nine months' space, brilliant deed,
> At the sound of Boirche's hen.

Also in BB. 399 a 32; H. 58 a; Lec. 506 b; and Rennes 116 a 2, where the "nine months" is reduced to "three fortnights". See, too, *Silva Gadelica*, ii, 531.

Ard Fothaid. This seems the same as the *Ard Fothadh* of the Four Masters, A.D. 639, "the name of a fort on a hill near Ballymagrorty .... in the co. of Donegal" (?). See also Reeves, *Vita Columbae*, p. 38, *note*. It is spelt *Ard Fothaid* in the *Tripartite Life*, Rolls ed., p. 148, and *Ardd Fothid* in the Book of Armagh, fo. 18 b 2.

Fothad Airgthech, a son of Mac-con, was slain in battle A.D. 285. There is a story about the identification of his tomb in LU. 133 b, which is printed and translated in Petrie's *Round Towers*, pp. 107, 108. The allusion to Boirche's hen is to me obscure.

[61. ARD MACHA.]—Ard Macha, cid dia ta? Ni *ansa*.
Macha ben Nemidh m*ei*c Agnomain atbath ann, ꝫ ba he in dara magh deg roslecht la Nemhead, ꝫ do breatha dia mhnai go mbeith a ainm uasa, ꝫ i ad*ch*o*nn*airc i n-aislinge foda reimhe a te*cht* ina ndernad do ulc im Thain bho Cuailngi ina cotludh tarfas di uile ann rocesad do ulc and do d*r*oibhelaib ꝫ do midhrennaib, go romhuidh a c*r*idhe inti. Un*de* Ard Macha.

Nó Macha ingen Ædha Ruaidh m*ei*c Baduirnn, is le rotoirneadh Eo-[fo. 5ᵃ 1]-muin¹ Macha, ꝫ is and roadnacht día ros-marbh Re*ch*taid² Rígderg, is dia gubhu rognídh ænach Macha. Un*de* Macha m*agh*.

Ailit*er*, Macha da*no* bean Cruind m*ei*c Agnomhain doriacht ann do comrith ann ri heocho C*on*chobair, ar atb*ert* a fear ba luathe a bean inaid na heocho. Amlaidh da*no* bai in bean sin, inbhadach, go ro chuindigh cairde go ro thæd abru, ꝫ ní tugadh di, ꝫ dogní in comhrith iarum ꝫ ba luaithiamh si, ꝫ o roshiacht cend in chede be*r*id mac ꝫ ingin, Fir ꝫ Fíal a n-anmann, ꝫ atb*ert* go mbeidis Ulaidh fo cheas³ oitedh in gach uair dos-figead eigin, *con*id de baí in cheas f*or* Ultu f*ri* re nomaide⁴ o re C*on*chobair go fla*ith* Mail m*ei*c Rocraide, ꝫ adb*er*ar ba si G*r*ian Banchu*re* ingean Midhir B*ri* L*éith*, ꝫ

---

¹ MS. i*m*ui. ² MS. rosumarb rechtaig. ³ MS. inserts ꝫ. ⁴ MS. xxᵈᵉ.

The Edinburgh Dinnshenchas.

adbeb iar suidhiu ⁊ focreas a *fert* i nArd Macha, ⁊ focer a gubha, ⁊ roclannad a lía. Un*de* Ard Macha.

> Atc*h*onnairc Ma*ch*a marglic
> t*r*i fhis, ratha na raidmid,
> tuirthe*ch*ta t*r*imsa Cuailghne
> fa gnim ndimsa nimuaibre.

Ard Macha, whence is it?

Not hard (to say). Macha, wife of Nemed, son of Agnoman, died there, and it was the twelfth plain which was cleared by Nemed, and it was bestowed on his wife that her name might be over it, and 'tis she that saw in a dream, long before it came to pass, all the evil that was done in the Driving of the Kine of Cualnge. In her sleep there was shown to her all the evil that was suffered therein, and the hardships and the wicked quarrels: so that her heart broke in her. Whence *Ard Macha*, "Macha's Height."

> Macha, the very shrewd, beheld
> Through a vision—graces which we say not—
> Descriptions of the times (?) of Cualgne—
> Twas a deed of pride, not of boasting.

Or, Macha, daughter of Aed the Red, son of Badurn: 'tis by her that Emain Macha was marked out, and there she was buried when Rechtaid Red-arm killed her. To lament her *Oenach Macha*, "Macha's Assembly," was held. Whence *Macha Magh*.

Aliter. Macha, now, wife of Crunn, son of Agnoman, came there to run against the horses of King Conor. For her husband had declared that his wife was swifter than the horses. Thus then was that woman pregnant: so she asked a respite till her womb had fallen, and this was not granted to her. So then she ran the race, and she was the swiftest. And when she reached the end of the green she brings forth a boy and a girl—Fír and Fíal were their names—and she said that the Ulaid would abide under debility of childbed whensoever need should befall them. So thence was the debility on the Ulaid for the space of five days and four nights (at a time) from the era of Conor to the reign of Mál, son of Rochraide (A.D. 107). And 'tis said that she was Grian Banchure, "the Sun of Womanfolk," daughter of Midir of Brí Léith. And after this she died, and her tomb was raised on Ard Macha, and her lamentation was made, and her pillar-stone was planted. Whence is *Ard Macha*, "Macha's Height."

Also in BB. 400 b 49; H. 61 b; Lec. 510 b; and R. 117 b 1. But none of these copies contain the account of the first Macha's dream, or the quatrain referring thereto. That the second Macha marked out Emain is told also in Cormac's Glossary, and LL. 20 b 48. The story of the third Macha's race with Conor's horses, and of the birth of her twins, is related more fully in LL. 125 b 42, whence it has been published by the late Sir Samuel Ferguson in a note to his *Congal*, pp. 189, 190, with a Latin version, and by Prof. Windisch in the *Berichte* of the Royal Saxon Gesellschaft der Wissenschaften, 1884, pp. 336-347, with a German translation.

[62. MAG COBA.]—Mag Coba, cid día ta? Ni *ansa*.
Mag Coba cuthchaire. *Nó* Coba cuthchaire feisin .i. cuthchaire Eremoin me*i*c Míleadh, is e cé*t*na roindlestair cuithigh i nEr*inn*. Atnaigh a chois indi d*us* in bad doith ina cuithigh, go romuidh buinde a sliasta ┐ a da dhoid, *con*-ablad de. Is de sin ata Mag Cobha. Un*de* poeta di*x*it :

> Cobha cuthcaire go ngloir
> ardri[g] Erend Eremhoin,
> is e rosdeadhlad de
> Coba cennmhar cuthchaire.

Mag Coba, whence is it?
Not hard to say. The plain of Coba the pitfall-maker. Or, Coba the pitfall-maker himself, that is, the pitfall-maker of Eremon, son of Míl. He first in Erin arranged a pitfall. And he put his foot into it to see whether it was . . . in his pitfall, whereupon his thighbone (?) broke, and his two forearms, so that he died thereof. Thence is *Mag Coba*, and hence the poet said :

> Coba the glorious pitfall-maker,
> Of Erin's over-king Eremon :
> 'Tis he that would sever himself from him,
> Great-headed Coba the pitfall-maker.

Also in BB. 400 b 34 ; H. 61 b; Lec. 510 b ; and Rennes 117 a 2.
Mag Coba seems to have been the old name for a portion of the baronies of Iveagh in Ulster. See Reeves, *Eccl. Antiquities of Down, Conor, and Dromore*, p. 349, where *cuthchaire* is misrendered by "huntsman".
As to Eremon, son of Míl, see the *Four Masters*, A.M. 3501, and *infra*, No. 76.

[63. SLIAB CALLAINN.]—Sliab Kallan, cid dia ta? Ni *ansa*.
Callann *con*bhuachaill Buidhe me*i*c Bain blaidh me*i*c Fo*r*gamhna fo*r*obar[t] in Don*n* Cuailghni in mi riana re coir .i. dairi int[s]easgraidhi imbi forrobartar ┐ in cu [oc cosnam in tsesc*r*aigh co torcair in cu di sodain—*BB*.] *Nó* gomadh ig taba*ir*t na tana comcomult in choin arin talamh. Un*de* Sliab Kalland.

> Calland *con*bhuachaill c*r*ethaigh [leg. crethaidh?]
> Buidhe mac Bain bithbreathaig.
> glecais f*r*issin nDonn Cuailghne
> ba fo*r*lonn f*r*i heduailghne [leg. étuailngi?].

Sliab Callann, whence is it?
Not hard (to say). Callann the sheep-dog of Buide, son of Ban blaith, son of Forgamuin. The Donn of Cualgne, the month before his proper time, proceeded to bull the dry cows around him. He and the dog began to contend for the dry cows, till the dog fell by him. Or it may be that at the taking the drove he crushed the dog on the ground. Whence *Sliab Callann*.

The Edinburgh Dinnshenchas.

Callann, the skilful (?) sheep-dog
Of Buide, son of ever-judging Ban,
Fought with the Brown Bull of Cualgne.
He was savage at wrong.

Also in BB. 404 b 1; H. 64 b; Lec. 514 b; and R. 119 b 2, where there is an additional paragraph stating that the dog was a pup of Daol, the hound of Celtchar, which had been found in the skull of Conganchnes ("Hornskin"), along with the hounds of Culann the Brazier and Mac dá Thó. As to this see the note in the left margin of LU. 61 a.

The Edinburgh codex is here so corrupt and incomplete that I have not ventured to punctuate, and my version is merely tentative.

Sliab Callann is now Slieve Gallion, a mountain in the county of Londonderry, on the borders of Tyrone.

The Donn of Cualgne (now Cooley in the co. of Louth) is the famous brown bull to obtain which was the object of the expedition known as the *Táin bó Cualngi*, "Driving of the kine of Cualnge."

[64. SLIAB FUAIT.]—Sliab Fuait, canas rohainmniged?
Fuad mac Bile meic Breoghain, is é robo rí Ua mBreoghain. Taraill inse[1] ar in fairrge [oc tuidecht la macaib Miled] dochum nErend, ⁊ gach æn nofuirmheadh a bond fuirri ni abrad gaí nó breig. Tug fod fírindi lais [fo. 5ᵃ 2] asin indsi. intan adbereadh gai dochuiredh[2] a fæsgul suas, ⁊ intan atberead firindi dochuireadh a chain suas. Ata in fod sin isin tshleib beus, ⁊ is fair dorochair in graindi o gherran Padraic, conidh adrad sruith[i] ardaigh na firinde do choimhet. Unde Sliabh Fuait.

Nó gomad in [leg. ón] fod doradad for Ceand mBerridi do imarchur, ar rothairgsead Ulaid righe don ænfhir noberadh corp Conchobhair go hEamain oda Mag Lamhraidhe gen fhuirmeadh, go rogabh Ceann Berride fair, go roisead Sliabh Fuait, go tarda bonn fri lár i Sleib Fuait. Adbertadar Ulaid na bad rí aire sin e. Atbert som fod go leithead a bonn do thabairt fair. Doradadh on go roacht Emhain. Conid ann dobhath, conidh desin ata "righe Chind Berride".

Fuat mac Bile chæimh cruadhaigh,[3]
ua Breaguin buirr bithbuadaig,[4]
tuc ar rod fear luchta ille
fod fors'tuc[tha] firinde.

Sliab Fuait, whence was it named?

Fuat, son of Bile, son of Breogan, 'tis he that was king of Húi Breogain. As he was coming to Erin with the sons of Míl he landed on an island in the ocean, and no one who set his sole thereon would utter a lie or a falsehood. Out of the island he brought a *fót* (sod) of truth, whereon he sat when dealing doom and deciding questions. When he uttered falsehood it would put

---

[1] For *inse* the MS. has (corruptly) for in fairgecht.   [2] Here the MS. inserts: a chain suas ata in fod.   [3] MS. cruaghaigh.
[4] MS. bithbuagaig.

its earthy side upwards, and when he uttered truth it would put its grassy side upwards. That sod is still on the mountain, and 'tis on it the single grain fell from St. Patrick's nag. Wherefore sages honour it because of preserving the truth.

Or it may be from the *fót* (sod) which was put upon Cenn Berridi to be carried; for the Ulaid had promised the realm to the one man who should carry (King) Conor's corpse from Magh Lamraide to Emain without laying it down. So Cenn Berridi took it up and reached Sliab Fuait, and on Sliab Fuait he put his sole to the ground. For that reason the Ulaid declared that he should not be king. He told them to put upon him a sod as broad as his sole. This was done, and he got to Emain, but there he (straightway) died. Whence is (the proverb), "Cenn Berride's Kingdom."

> Fuat, son of dear hardy Bilè,
> Grandson of rough, ever-victorious Breogan,
> The man of the burden brought hither on a road
> A sod whereon truth was put.

Also in BB. 404 a 31; Lec. 514 a; and R. 119 b 2, where the name of the island is given as *Inis Magdena*, or *Moagdeda*, id est *mór*, *óg*, *diada*, "great, perfect, divine"; and where the mountain's name is also derived from that of Fuat. See also *Silva Gadelica*, ii. 521.

H. adds the story of Cenn Berridhe. See as to this LL. 124 a 32-37, and O'Mahony's *Keating*, p. 273.

Emain, now the Navan Fort, near Armagh. *Sliab Fuait*, a mountain near Newtown Hamilton, in the county of Armagh.

Other ancient Irish ordeals are described in *Irische Texte*, 3. Serie, 1 Heft, pp. 185 *et seq.*

The story of the grain of wheat is told in the *Tripartite Life*, Rolls ed., p. 240.

[65. LIA LINDGADAIN.]—Lia Lindghadain, cid dia ta?

Li[n]gadan Labar, issé no chosced slú]agh Er*enn* i flaith Find me*i*c Findtain, ┐ ni lamtha labhrad leis f*or* muir na for tír gan íarfaighidh do son, ar is e robo sluag-re*ch*taire f*er* nEr*enn*. Rolabrasdar fe*cht* n-and f*r*ia di chulaidh asin carraig [in] m*a*c alla a gotha. Imsai[1] f*r*is anall do dhighail a gotha fair. Dan-arraidh barr[2] na murthuinde ┐ ran-esart f*r*isin carraig, *con*idh romarbh fodiadh.[3] is and bai ceand a shæghail. Un*de* dictum est:

> Linga labor, fear go mblaid,
> robai i n-aimsir Fhindtain.
> rofæn in[fh]airrgi go foll
> ria thæbh chairrgi gan chomhlaind.

Lia Lingadain, whence is it?

Lingadan the Arrogant, 'tis he that used to control the host of Erin in the reign of Find, son of Finntan, and no one durst

---

[1] MS. imrai.   [2] MS. danearraidh bara.   [3] MS. fodiagh.

speak with him, on sea or on land, without being asked by him, for he was the host-steward of the men of Erin. Once upon a time the echo of his (own) voice spoke out of the crag behind him. He turned towards it to take vengeance upon it for speaking, and the crest of the sea-wave overtook him and dashed him against the crag, so that, finally, he died. There was the end of his life. Whence was said:

> Linga the Arrogant, a man with fame,
> Lived in the time of Finntan,
> The sea threw him backwards violently,[1]
> Against the side of a crag, without conflict.

Also in LL. 165 b 25; BB. 407 b 3; H. (I omitted to note the page); and Lec. 519 b.
Of "Find, son of Finntan", I know nothing.

[66. MAG MUGNA.]—Magh Mughna, canas rohainmnigheadh? Maighnia *nó* Mairgnia .i. morgnimh feadha daurbhile mora roasai ann, comtír coimhleathna a mbarr f*r*issin magh. teora toirthi fodocheardais in gach blia*dain* [.i. dearcain ⁊ ubla ⁊ cnai.] Intan dothuitead in dearcu dedhenach is and nofhasadh blaith na ce[t]derca*n* dib, *com*dh taibhdeisdear Ninne eigeas, go ro leagh riamh *con*de*r*gan ailind de .i. níth nemhannach, ⁊ is desin ata Magh Mugna.

> Mughna durbhile gan on
> f*or*sa mbid meas is torudh.
> ba comhleathan a barr be*cht*
> f*r*isin magh mor gan eigeart .i. aine orda.

Mag Mughna, whence was it named?
Maighnia or *mair-gnia*, "great sister's son," to wit, a great deed. *Here there is a lacuna.*
Woods, great oak-trees grew there, so that their tops were as broad as the plain. Three fruits they used to yield in every year, to wit, acorns and apples, and nuts. When the last acorn fell, then the blossom of the first of these acorns would grow, so that Ninine the poet . . . .
and thence is Magh Mugna.

> Mughna's oak-tree without blemish,
> Whereon were mast and fruit,
> Its top was as broad precisely
> As the great plain without . . . .

Also in BB. 368 b 26; H. 23 a; Lec. 466 a; and R. 101 b. All the copies are obscure, and the Edinburgh copy is incomplete.
In a note to the *Calendar of Oengus*, Dec. 11, Mugna is said to have been a

---

[1] This line is a mere guess. I take *rofaen* to be 3rd sg. pret. of a denominative from *faen* = Lat. *supinus*, and *foll* to be *oll* .i. mór (O'Cl.), with prothetic *f*. The compar. *f-ulliu* occurs in LU. 22ᵇ 40.

The Edinburgh Dinnshenchas.

tree 30 cubits in girth and 300 cubits in height, which bore fruit thrice a year, and remained hidden from the Deluge till the birth of Conn of the Hundred Battles. And in LL. 200 a 12, we read that it fell southwards over Mag n-Ailbi, that it bore 900 sacks of acorns, and yielded three crops every year—"apples, wonderful, marvellous; nuts, round, blood-red; and acorns, brown, ridgy."

[67. FINDLOCH CERA.]—[fo. 5ᵇ 1] Find loch Cera, cid dia ta? Ni *ansa*.

Enlaith tiri tairngiri dodheachadar and do fhailte f*ri* Pad*r*aig dia mbai i Cruaich Aigle. Rofearsat gles fo*r*sin loch goma findithir lemn*acht*, ⁊ rochansat ceol ann gen bhai Padraic fo*r*sin cruaich. C*o*nidh de sin ata Findloch Ceara. Doluidhset tar muir alle enlaith tire tairngire gor gellsad in loch darlibh i coindi Padraig portghil.

Findloch ["White Lake"] of Cera, whence is it?

Not hard (to say). A flock of birds of the Land of Promise came there to welcome St. Patrick when he was on Cruach Aigle. They struck the lake (with their wings) till it was white as new milk, and they sang music there so long as Patrick remained on the Cruach. So thence is Findloch ("White-lake") of Cera. The birds of the Land of Promise fared hither over sea. . . . .

Also in H. 44 b; Lec. 487 a; and R. 112 b 2. Versified LL. 158 b. The last sentence I cannot translate.

Findloch Cera, now Lough Carra, in the co. of Mayo.
The Land of Promise, one of the Irish names for Fairyland.
Cruach Aigle, now Croaghpatrick in Connaught.

[68. MAG TAILTEN.]—Mag Tailden, cid dia ta? Ni *ansa*.

Tailltiu inghen Maghmhoir rig Espaine, ben Each*ach* Gairbh m*ei*c Duach Teimhin. Ba si mumi Loga m*ei*c Eithleann, ⁊ isi ro-claidheadh in magh. *Nó* is and atbath. Dia taide fogumhair roladh a fe*r*t ⁊ doronadh a gubha ⁊ ro*acht* a[1] nasad la Lugh [unde Lugnasa(d) dicimus. Coic cet bliadan im*morro* ⁊ mili ria ngein Crist andsin, ⁊ nognithe ind ænach la cach ríg nogeibed Eiri co tainic Patraic, ⁊ coic cet aenach i Tailltin o Patraic co Duboenach Dondchada (meic Flaind) meic Mail-sechlainn]. *Ocus* it e teora gesa Tailtean : te*cht* tairse gen tairleim, a deagsain tara ghualaind clí ig taidhe*cht*[2] uaithi, faisdibhrugudh fu*i*rri iar fuineadh ngreine. Un*de* Magh T*ailten*.

   Tailltiu ingean Magmhoir mhoill,
   is i sin ro ben in choill,
   bumi Logha luaidhit fir,
   baile in teidi-sea im Thailltin.

Mag Tailten, whence is it?

Not hard (to say). Tailltiu, daughter of Maghmor, King of

---

[1] *an* erased.   [2] MS. taighecht.

The Edinburgh Dinnshenchas.

Spain, wife of Eochaid the Rough, son of Dua the Dark-grey. She was Lugh mac Ethlenn's foster-mother, and 'tis she that used to dig the plain.¹ Or 'tis there that she died. On the first day of autumn her tomb was built, and her lamentation was made and her funeral game was held by Lugh [whence we say *Lughnasadh*, " Lammastide". Five hundred years and a thousand before Christ's birth was that, and that assembly was held by every king who took Ireland until Patrick came, and there were five hundred assemblies in Tailtiu from Patrick down to the Black Assembly of Donnchad, son of Flann, son of Maelsechlainn]. And these are the three tabus of Tailtiu: crossing it without alighting; looking at it over one's left shoulder when coming from it; idly casting at it after sunset. Whence *Magh Tailten*, " Taltiu's Plain."

> Taltiu, slow Magmor's daughter,
> 'Tis she that cut down the forest.
> Lugh's foster-mother, men declare,
> The place of this assembly (is) round Tailtiu.

Also in BB. 403 a 30; H. 10 b; Lec. 513 a; and R. 119 a 1, from which the words in brackets have been taken. See also *Silva Gadelica*, ii, 514.

Tailtiu, now Teltown, in Meath. For traditions relating to the assembly or fair held there, see O'Mahony's *Keating*, p. 301, and the *Four Masters*, A.M. 3370.

The above etymology of *Lughnasadh* is also in Cormac's Glossary.

Donnchad, son of Flann Sinna, son of Mael-shechlainn, was over-king of Ireland from A.D. 918 to A.D. 942. The " Black Assembly" means, perhaps, the assembly which, in A.D. 925, was prevented by Muirchertach, son of Niall.

[69. BENN BAIRCHI.]—Beand Bairchi, cidh dia ta? Ni *ansa*.
.1. Bairche boaire Rosa Ruaidhbuidhi, ba headh a shuidhi mbuachalla, in bheand, ⁊ is cuma argairead gach mboin oda Dun Sobairce go rige in mBoaind, ⁊ ni geilead mil dib mír *for*oil seach araile, *con*aidh desin ata Beand Bairchi, am*ail* asbe*rt* :

> Bairchi boaire gu mbladh²
> baí ag Rosa [leg. Ross] Ruadh roneartmhar
> in beand, nach tlaith re duba,
> a suidhi blaith buachalla.

Benn Bairchi, whence is it?

Not hard (to say). Bairche, Ross Ruddy-yellow's cowherd, this was his herdsman's seat, the Benn, and (there) equally would he herd every cow from Dunseverick to the Boyne: and no (one) beast of them would graze a bit in excess of another. So thence is *Benn Bairchi*, " Bairche's Peak," as said (the poet):

---

¹ *I.e.*, to dig up the roots of the trees with which the plain was covered.   ² MS. mblaidh.

Bairche, the famous cowherd,
Who belonged to very mighty Ross the Red:
The peak was the soft seat of the herdsman,
Who was not weak against sadness.

Also in BB. 403 a; H. 64 a; Lec. 512 b; and R. 118 b 2. See also *Silva Gadelica*, ii, 527. BB., H., and Lec. add the following:
Aliter, Be*n*nan mac mBricc, hind romarb Ibel mac Manannan i ndul coa mhnai .1. Leccon i*ngen* Lodair a hainm sen, *con*id he sin fath darroleic Manan*nan* a t*ri* lom*n*iand cumad dia c*r*idiu .1. Loch Ruide, L*och* Cuan, L*och* Dachæch, 7 romarb Bendan iarsin f*or* a benn ut. Unde Benn B*ennain* dicitur.
"Otherwise: Bennan, son of Brec: thereon he killed Ibel, son of Manannan, for going to his wife, whose name was Leccon, daughter of Lodar. So this was the cause why Manannan cast from his heart his three draughts of grief, (which became) Loch Ruide, Strangford Lough, Waterford Harbour. And he afterwards killed Bennan on yon peak. Hence it is called *Benn Bennain*, " Bennan's Peak."
Beanna Boirche, the Peaks of Boirche, "is still applied to that part of the Mourne Mountains, in the county of Down, in which the river Bann has its source," *Four Masters*, 1493, note *j*.
Loch Ruide not identified.
Ross Ruad-buide (or *Rigbuide*, "yellow-forearmed"), King of Ulaid in the third century.

[70. Traig Tuirbi.]—Traig Tuirbe, cidh dia ta? Ni *ansa*.
Turbe T*r*aghmar, athair Gobain sair, [is e rodon-seilb. Is on forbbai—*BB*.] is e focheirdeadh a urchur dia biail[1] i[2] Telaigh Bela inaghaidh in tuile, *co n*-ergaradh in fairrgi [┐ ni tuidchead tairis—*BB*.]. *Ocus* ni feas a geinelach[3] *acht* masa dinibh teasbadhchaibh æsa dana atrulliath a Temraigh ria Sam-ildanach fail i ndiamraib Breagh. Un*de* T*ráig* T*uirbe*.

Tuirbe trágmar[4] ba fear feimh,[5]
athair Gobain go nglainmhein,
ni fes a geinelach[6] gle:
uad ainmnigt*her* T*r*aig Turbe.

Tráig Tuirbi, whence is it?
Not hard (to say). Tuirbe Trágmar, father of Gobbán the Wright, 'tis he that owned it. 'Tis from that heritage he, (standing) on Telach Bela ("the Hill of the Axe"), would hurl a cast of his axe in the face of the floodtide, so that he forbade the sea, which then would not come over the axe. And his pedigree is not known, unless he be one of the defectives of the men of art who fled out of Tara before Samildánach, (and whose posterity) is in the secret parts of Bregia. Whence *Tráig Tuirbi*, "Turbe's Strand."

---

[1] MS. biailli. [2] MS. ai. [3] MS. geinedhlach. [4] MS. tradmar.
[5] *feimh* [leg. *féimh?*] negligent, neglectful, O'Reilly. [6] MS. geineadhlach.

The Edinburgh Dinnshenchas.

Tuirbe Trágmar was a negligent man,
Father of Gobbán with pure desire.
Unknown is his bright pedigree,
From him Tráig Tuirbi is named.

Also in BB. 408 b; H. 68 a; Lec. 520 b; and R. 124 b 1. See also Petrie's *Round Towers*, pp. 382, 383; O'Curry's *Manners and Customs*, iii, 41; and O'Grady's *Silva Gadelica*, ii, 518.

According to Petrie, *Tráig Tuirbi* is now Turvey, on the northern coast of the co. of Dublin, and the *Diamra Breagh* are now Diamor in Meath.

The *Gobbán Saer* was an architect who flourished (according to Petrie) early in the seventh century.

Samildánach, "skilled-in-many-arts-together," συμπολύτεχνος, if one may coin a Greek word, was a name for Lugh mac Ethlenn. See "The Second Battle of Moytura", *Rev. Celtique*, xii, pp. 74, 76, 78, 80.

The tale of Tuirbe and his axe is a tolerably close parallel to that of Paraçurâma. "This hero, after the destruction of the Kshatriya race, bestowed the earth upon the Brâhmans, who repaid the obligation by banishing him as a homicide from amongst them. Being thus at a loss for a domicile, he solicited one of the ocean, and its regent-deity consented to yield him as much land as he could hurl his battle-axe[1] along. Paraçurâma threw the weapon from Gokernam to Kumâri, and the retiring ocean yielded him the coast of Malabar, below the latitude of 15°," H. H. Wilson, *Catalogue of the Mackenzie Collection*, 2nd ed., Madras, 1882, p. 56.

So in his *Glossary of Judicial and Revenue Terms*, London, 1855, p. 401: "PARAÇURAMA . . . . An avatar of Vishṅu, to whom is ascribed the recovery from the sea of Kerala, or Malabar, by casting his axe from a point of the coast, Mount Dilli . . . . to the extreme south; the sea retiring from the part over which the axe flew."

[71. LUSMAG.]—Lusmag, cid dia ta? Ni *ansa*.

IS as tug Dianccht ga*ch* l*u*s n-íce conammalt ar[2] thip*r*ait Slain[gi i n-Achad Abla] f*r*i Mag T*ui*red aniarthuaith, intan bai cath *etir* T*u*atha De Danann [fo. 5ᵇ 2] ⁊ Fomhoire. [Gach aen do Thuatha*ib* De Da*n*a*nn* no laigtis fon lind l*u*sraid sin at*r*aiged slemun slanc*r*echtac[h]—*BB.*] Un*de* Lusmag.

> Diancecht dorat leis alle
> gach lus o Lusmhaigh luaidhe [leg. luaighne?],
> go tip*r*ait na slainti suaill
> f*r*i Magh Tuiread aniarthuaidh.[3]

Lusmag, whence is it?

Not hard (to say). 'Tis thence that Diancecht brought every herb of healing and grated them on Slainge's Well in Achad Abla, north-west of Moytura, when there was a battle between the Tuatha De Danann and the Fomorians. Every one of the Tuatha De Danann whom they would lay under that water of herbs would arise smooth and healed of his wounds. Whence *Lusmag*, "Herb-plain."

---

[1] *paraçu-s* = Gr. πέλεκυς, cognate perhaps with Welsh *elech*, "saxum".   [2] MS. ɔmſ a.   [3] MS. -thuaigh.

The Edinburgh Dinnshenchas.

Diancecht brought with him hither
Every herb from precious[1] Lusmag
To the well of the little healths,
North-west of Moytura.

Also in BB. 406 a; H. 44 b; Lec. 488 a; and R. 112 b 2.
Lusmag, " Herb-plain," now perhaps Lusmagh in King's County. The *Achad Abla*, " Field of the Apple-tree," here mentioned, has not, so far as I know, been identified. Northern *Magh Tuiredh*, the battlefield here mentioned, is now a townland in the barony of Tirerrell, co. of Sligo. For a romantic account of the battle, see *Revue Celtique*, xii, 56-110. The healing-well is mentioned *ibid.*, pp. 94, 96.

[72. BENN CODAIL.]—Beand Codhail can a[s] rohainmnigeadh? Ni *ansa*.
Codhol Coirrchicheach is e rob[2] aide do Eirind diata Inis Er*enn*, ⁊ is ann tairbreadh a dalta f*or* in beind ud, ⁊ nach tairb*er*t dobeiread f*ur*ri *con*ogbhadh in talamh foaib, ⁊ mairb*er*ead Eiriu atum*a*dar suas go tiagat a goth gæithe fu domhnaib a cluass man[i]abr*a*d (sí) sin ⁊ nofhasfadh gomadh reil Eire uile as, ⁊ an la domela comarba Er*enn* no rí Temrach tuara Codhail *nó* ní d'enlaith *nó* d'fíaduch[3] *nó* di iasc, f*or*br*a*id a ghal ⁊ a slainte. Un*de* Beand Codhail.

        Codhal Coirrchicheach go n-aibh
        topghais Erind abradchain,
        manbadh Eriu cæmh monur
        cia cia bad leiriu cæmhchodhul.

Benn Codail, whence was it named?
Not hard (to say). Codal, the Round-breasted, 'tis he that was fosterer to Eriu, from whom is the island of Erin, and on yon peak he used to feed (?) his fosterling, and with every . . . . he would put upon her the ground would rise up under them, and Eriu . . . . And the day that Erin's *coarb* (successor) or Tara's king shall partake of Codal's food, or aught of birds or venison or fish, his valour and his health increase. Whence *Benn Codail*, "Codal's Peak."

The rest of the prose, and the quatrain, are so corrupt and obscure in the Edinburgh codex and the other MSS. (BB. 406 a; H. 13 b; L. 516 a; and R. 121 a 1) that I do not venture to translate them.
Benn Codail has not been identified.
Eriu is perhaps the queen of the Tuatha Dé Danann, mentioned in LL. 10 a, and O'Mahony's *Keating*, pp. 82, 141, 198.

[73. TLACHTGA.]—Tlachtgha canas rohainmnigheadh? Ni *ansa*.
Tlachtgha ingean Mogha[4] Roith f*or*dos-reibleangadar t*r*i m*e*ic Simoin druadh[5] dia luidh le hat[h]air da foglaim druidhe*ch*t*a* i

---

[1] luaigne . 1. logmar, O'Dav.   [2] MS. romb.   [3] MS. dfiaguch, the
f inserted by the corrector.   [4] MS. modha.   [5] MS. druagh.

n-airth*iur* in betha, fodeigh is i doroighni in Roth Ramach do
Th*ri*un ⁊ in lia i F*or*carthu ⁊ in coir[th]i i Cnamhchaill. Ternai
iaramh anair [⁊] in dedha sin le go torr*acht* tealaigh Tla*cht*ga.
Fordos-lamnad annsin iarum go mb*er*dais t*ri* ma*cc*u .i. Doirb,
dia ta Magh nDoirbi, ⁊ Cuma, dia ta Magh Cuma, ⁊ Múach, dia ta
Magh Mu[a]ich. I cein da*no* beid in[na] anmand sin i cuimni
fear nEr*enn* ní thora dígal n-e*cht*rann docum nEr*enn*. O*cus*
atbath dia hassaid,[1] ⁊ is uirri dorindeadh in dun. Un*de* Tlachtga.

> Tlachtga inghen Modha moir
> ros-lebhlan[g]adar me*ic* Simoin.
> onn uair thanic dar muir mas
> is di ata Tla*cht*gha tæbghlas.

Tlachtga, whence was it named?

Not hard (to say). Tlachtga, daughter of Mogh Ruith, three
sons of Simon Magus ravished her when she went with her
father to learn wizardry in the eastern part of the world, because
'tis she that had made the Rowing Wheel for Trian (?) and the
Stone in Forcarthu, and the Pillar-stone in Cnámchoill.

Then she escaped from the east, bringing those two things with
her till she reached the hill of Tlachtga. There, then, she lay in,
and three sons were born, to wit, Doirb, from whom Mag nDoirbe
(is named), Cumma, from whom is Mag Cumma, and Muach, from
whom is Mag Muaich. So long as these names shall remain
in the memory of the men of Erin, foreigners' vengeance shall not
visit Ireland. And she died in childbed, and over her the
fortress was built, whence *Tlachtga*.

> Tlachtga, daughter of great Mogh,
> Simon's sons ravished her.
> From the hour that she came over the beautiful sea
> After her green-sided Tlachtga is (named).

Also in BB. 406 b; H. 13 b; Lec. 516 b; and R. 121 a. See also *Silva Gadelica*, ii, 511.

Tlachtga is now the Hill of Ward, near Athboy in Meath, *Four Masters*, A.D. 1172, note *i*, and *Book of Rights*, p. 10, note *t*.

Forcarthu is near Rathcoole and *Cnámchaill* in Tipperary.

As to the wizard Mogh Ruith and the Rowing Wheel, which is to roll over Europe before Doomsday, see the Bodleian MS. Laud 610, fo. 109 a 1, and O'Curry's *Lectures*, pp. 272, 385, 401, 421, 423, 428. Of the Pillar-stone of Cnámchoill it is said in Laud 610, fo. 109 a 2: Dall cach oen notn-aicfe, bodar cach oen nod-cluinfe, marb cach óen risi mbenfa. "Blind (will be) every one who shall see it; deaf every one who shall hear it; and dead every one against whom it shall strike."

Mag Cumma (in Húi Neill, *Four Masters*, A.M. 3529), like *Mag nDoirbe* and *Mag Muaich*, is now unknown.

[74. INBER CICHMAINI.]—INb*er* Cichmaine can as rohainmnigheadh? Ni *ansa*.

---

[1] MS. hassaidh.

The Edinburgh Dinnshenchas.

Cich-maine[1] Adhnai mac Ailella ⁊ Meadhbha, ar ba Maine Adnai in sech*t*mad mac do Ai*l*i*l*l ⁊ do Meidhbh, ut sup*r*a diximu*s*. IS e da*no* in Maine sin fo*rr*uidbigh Feargna mac Finnchoime oc cosnam[2] churaigh fo*r*sin tracht.

Nó Cichmuine mac Ai*l*ella find fuaradar araile iasgaire ic telach[3] [al lin ⁊ a cocholl, coro marbsat isin inb*iu*r (ucut). .Unde In*b*er Cic*h*maini.]

In*b*er Cichmaini, whence was it named?
Not hard (to say). Cich-maine Adnoe, son of Ailill and Medb, for Maine Adnoe was the seventh son of Ailill and Medb, as we said above. 'Tis that Maine, then, that Fergna, son of Findchoem, slew (?) while contending for a boat on the strand.

Or Cich-maine, son of Ailill the Fair, certain fishermen found loosing their nets and their hoods.[4] So they killed him in yon estuary, and hence *Inber Cichmaini* is named.

<small>Also in BB. 405 a; H. 12 a; L. 515 a; and R. 120 a 2. From R. the words in brackets have been taken.
Inber Cichmaini has not, so far as I know, been identified. O'Curry, *Manners and Customs*, iii, 162, 188, says it is on the east coast of Ulster. Etain was reared there, LU. 129 a 23.</small>

(Egerton 1781, fo. 75b.)

[75. Loch Cé.]—Loch Cé, can*us* rohainmnighe*d*h?
Ni *ansa*. Cé .i. d*r*ái Nuadha*t* Airge*t*laim me*i*c E*ch*taigh me*i*c Ete*r*laim rotáet a *cath* M*ai*ge T*ur*edh iarna guin isin cath co rainic Carn Coirrsléb*h*i ⁊ co rainic in Magh Airni a fuil in loch, ⁊ docer Cáe ann sin, *con*id ica idhnacal ro meb*ai*d*h* in lo*ch*. Un*de* Loch Cé.

Loch Cé, whence was it named?
Not hard (to say). Cé, the wizard of Nuada Silverhand, entered the battle of Magh Turedh. Having been wounded in the fight, he went to Corrshlébhe, and (then) he went to Magh Airni, where the lake is. And there Cé fell, and at his burial the lake burst forth. Whence is *Loch Cé*, "Cé's Lake."

<small>Also in H. 66 b; and Lec. 490. Edited (with a translation) from the latter MS. by Hennessy, in the preface to his *Annals of Loch Cé*, pp. xxxvi-xxxix. The copy in H. 66 b has never been published, and is as follows:</small>

Loch Ce, can*as* ro*ainmniged*?
Ni *ansa*. Antan rofechta cath Muighi Tuiredh eter Fomorchaib et Toatha D*e* D*a*n*a*n*n*, rogonadh dno ann drui Nuadat Arccetlaim m*a*ic E*ch*ta*i*g a fritguin an imair[i]g. Cé a ainm-s*id*e. La sodain doriecht roimi sierdes on muigh co torracht Carn

---

<small>[1] MS. ciachmhaine.   [2] MS. finnchoinne ochosnam.   [3] telach .i. sgaoileadh, O'Clery.   [4] *cocholl*, borrowed from Lat. *cucullus*. P. O'Connell has *cochall*, a net, a fishing net.</small>

The Edinburgh Dinnshenchas.

Corrslébe, co ndeissed as-suid*iu* iar scis ghona et uamain ⁊ im-
te*ch*tai *acht* chena is suaill nar 'bo marb focetoir. asiu rofaccadh in
carn forar' dheiss*ed*. Rosill uaid sairtuaidh ca*ch*ndireach co facca
in mag minscothach. Ba lainn lais rochtain an muighe atconnairc.
Luid rome for an amth*as* fon ind*us* sin co larmhedón in muighe,
ait a mbui carrac cobs*aid*h comadb*ul*, conadh [ón] drai rohainm-
nigthe .i. Carrac Ce, *con*adh fon cairn roladh fo talmain iarna
eibelt. Intan iarum roclas a f*er*t is ann [ba] tomaidm an locha
taris et tar[s]in magh olchena. Unde Loch Ce.

Loch Cé, whence was it named?
Not hard (to say). When the battle of Magh Tuiredh was
fought between the Fomorians and the Tuatha Dé Danann the
wizard of Nuada Silverhand, son of Echtach, was wounded there
in the brunt of the contest. Cé was his name. Thereat he
fared forward south-west from the plain till he reached Carn
Corrslébe, and sat down thereon (so) wearied with his wounding
and fear and travel, that he almost died forthwith. From this
was seen the cairn on which he sat. He looked due north-east,
and he saw the smooth and flowerful plain. Fain was he to
reach the plain that he saw. On he went on the . . . . in that
wise to the very centre of the plain, where there was a rock, firm
and huge, which was (afterwards) named from the wizard, to wit
Carrac Cé. And under the cairn he was interred after he had
perished. Now when his tomb was dug there was an outburst of
the lake over it, and over the rest of the plain. Whence is *Loch
Cé*.

Loch Cé, now Lough Key, is a lake in the county of Roscommon, near the
town of Boyle. *Corrshliabh*, the Curlew Mountains, also near Boyle.
As to the battle of Magh Tuiredh, see *supra*, No. 71, and *Rev. Celtique*, xii,
52 *et seq*.
As to Nuada and his silvern hand, *ibid.*, 58, 66; LL. 9 a, 127 a; and the
Four Masters, A.M. 3303.

[76. MAG NDUMACH.]—Magh nDumach, cidh dia ta?
Ni *ansa*. Cath dorata*d*h imna t*r*i d*r*uimn*ibh* ada de*ch* bái a
nEr*inn* .i. Druim C*r*ec*ht* [fo. 76ᵇ 2] ⁊ D*r*uim B*et*ach a *cu*it Eremoin
⁊ D*r*uim Fingin a *cu*it Eb*i*r. Ba bec la hEb*er* ænd*r*uim isin l*et*h
thes ⁊ a dó sa t*ir* tuaidh, ⁊ atbert Er*imon* na b*ad* athroin*n* uad dia
cuit. F*er*tar *cat*h etarru. Rom*eb*a*id* tra *for* Eb*er*, *con*dorcai*r* ann
Eb*er* ⁊ Palap m*ac* Er*emon* la C*on*mæl m*ac* Ca*th*bad, ⁊ rogníad
dumad[a] ar in læchra*id*h annsin. Un*de* Magh nDum*ach*, ⁊ Tendais a ainm ar t*us*. Un*de* d*i*c*itu*r:

San cath *for* Tenndais na t*r*eabh
sin muigh a dorchair Eb*er*,
a do*r*c*r*adar ann malle
Gois*t*in,[1] Sétga *ocus* Suirge.

---

[1] MS. gorestin.

The Edinburgh Dinnshenchas.

A tochar *etir* da magh
in cl. *fri* bothar n-air
E*ber* m*ac* Mile*d* cobe*cht*
is ed a l*eacht* anasb.

U*nde* M*ag* nDumach d*icit*[ur].

Magh nDumach, whence was it named?
Not hard (to say). A battle was there delivered (between Eber and Eremon, two sons of Míl) concerning the three ridges which were best in Ireland, to wit, Druim Crecht [Cresach—*L*. Clasaigh—*F. M.*] and Druim Bethach in Eremon's portion, and Druim Fingin in Eber's portion. To Eber it seemed petty to have one ridge in the southern half and two in the northern country. And Eremon said that there would be no repartition by him of his share. (So) a battle is fought between them. Eber was routed, and therein fell Eber and Palap, son of Eremon, by Conmael, son of Cathbad, and mounds were built over the heroes there, whence *Magh nDumach*, "the mounded Plain," and Tendais had been its name originally. Whence is said:

> In the battle on Tendais of the habitations,
> In the plain where Eber fell,
> There fell together
> Goisten, Sétga, and Suirge.[1]

> On a causeway between two plains
> . . . . . to the east of a road,
> Eber, son of Míl, certainly
> This is his grave . . . .

Also in Lec. 524 b, but, so far as I am aware, nowhere else.

Mag nDumach is perhaps the place called by the Four Masters, A D. 858, *Magh Duma*, which O'Donovan says is now called Moy, adjoining Charlemont, on the Tyrone side of the Blackwater.

As to Eber and Eremon and their dispute, see the *Four Masters*, A.M. 3501.

Druim Clasaigh is a long hill in Hy-Many, between Lough Ree and the river Suck. *Druim Beathaigh* was the name of a ridge across the plain of Maenmagh, near the town of Loughrea, in the county of Galway. *Druim Finghin* is a ridge extending from near Castle-Lyons in the co. of Cork to the south side of the Bay of Dungarvan.

[77. CNUCHA.]—Cnucha, can*as* rohainmnighedh?
Ni *ansa*. Dia tangat*ar* .u. m*eic* Dela m*eic* Loith cho Er*inn*, Gann ⁊ Genann ⁊ Rud*raige* ⁊ Sengann ⁊ Slaine, dorats*at* .u. righna leo .i. Fuat ben Slaine a quo (*sic*) nominatur Sl*iab*h Fuait ⁊ inisin Fuata, Etar b*en* Gainn, isí atbath i nEt*ur*, ⁊ is uaithi

---

[1] These were, according to the *Four Masters*, "three distinguished chieftains of the people of Eremon." I cannot translate the following quatrain.

The Edinburgh Dinnshenchas.

ainm*nigther* Etar, An*u*st be*n* Se*n*gainn, Lí ben Rud*r*aigi, Cnuca ben Genainn, is i *co*nap*aid* 'sin tilaig sin, ⁊ is inti roadhno*cht*, *co*nidh uaithi ainmnig*ther* Cnucha.

   Coig mna t*uc*satar aleth [leg. ille]
   coig me*ic* Del*a* can duilgi,
   da mnai dibh Cnucha co mbl*adh*
   is Et*ur* o t*rocht* imgl*an*.

   Atbath Cnucha sunna tra
   san cnuc ria n-abar Cnucha,
   atbath Et*ur* be*n* Gainn gluair
   a mBen[n] Et*air* re henuair.

   De sin ata Étar án
   is Cnucha cé*t*ach coml*án*,
   is inis Fuata can ail
   ocus Sl*iab*h Fuait co morbl*aidh*.

No Cnucha ingen Conn*aid*h a hiath*aib*h Luimn*ig*h, buime C*u*inn Cé*tcathaig* docoid ann do tham ina tigh fen [⁊ do hadhnaicedh la Connaidh (?) isin chnuc ugad .i. Cnucha. Unde Cnucha dicitur].

 Cnucha, whence was it named?
 Not hard (to say). When the five sons of Dela, son of Loth, came to Erin, (to wit) Gann, Genann, Rudraige, Sengann, and Sláine, they brought five queens with them, to wit, Fuat, Sláine's wife (from whom is named Sliab Fuait and Inis Fuata), Etar, Gann's wife—'tis she that died on Etar, and from her it is named—Anust, wife of Sengann, Lí, wife of Rudraige, and Cnucha, wife of Genann. 'Tis she that died on that hill, and therein she was buried. Wherefore from her Cnucha is named.

   Dela's five sons without trouble
   Brought hither five wives:
   Two of them were famous Cnucha
   And Etar from the very clear strand.

   Now Cnucha died here
   On the hill called Cnucha,
   And Etar, wife of pure Gann,
   On Benn Etair at the same hour.

   Thence is splendid Etar
   And Cnucha, the very full,
   And Inis Fuata without shame,
   And Sliab Fuait with great renown.

 Or Cnucha, daughter of Connad from the lands of Luimnech, fostermother of Conn of the Hundred Battles. She died there of the plague in her own house, [and she was buried by Conaing [leg. Connad?] in yon hill, namely, Cnucha. Whence *Cnucha* is said.

The last paragraph (but not the first, nor the verses) is contained in Lec. 525 a. I know of no other copy.

Cnucha is probably now Castleknock, near Dublin. See O'Donovan's note *f*, *Four Masters*, A.M. 3579.

As to the five sons of Dela, *ibid.*, A.M. 3266, and LL. 127 a. As to their wives, BB. 283 a 5-8.

Benn Etair, now Howth.

For *Sliab Fuait* a different etymology is given *supra*, No. 64. *Inis Fuata* not identified.

CORRIGENDA AND ADDENDA.

Folk-Lore, Vol. iii, pp. 470-516.

P. 470, l. 13, *read* Bregh[d]a.
,, l. 29, *for* Tea of Bregia *read* Bregian Tea.
P. 473, l. 10, *for* the *read* its.
P. 475, l. 4, *for* ónd *read* ón dub.
,, l. 19, *for* came *read* was let.
,, l. 22, *before* river *insert* dark.
P. 476, l. 15, *for* Hateful *read* A bad smoke; and in note 3, *for* from . . . *meiden*, *read* made up, for the nonce, from the prefix *mt-* and *dé* "smoke".
P. 481, l. 7, *for* in dail *read* ind ail.
,, l. 23, *for* beauty *read* defence (?).
,, l. 26, *for* worded doom *read* shameful word.
P. 482, l. 18, *after* an*nu* *insert* leg. a ndú.
,, l. 39, *for* to-day *read* (is) their place.
P. 483, l. 21, *for* breast *read* belly.
P. 484, l. 30, *after* Miandais *insert* leg. Anais.
P. 485, l. 5, *after* other *insert* (now Slievemish).
P. 486, l. 14, *after* Samaisce *insert* [Ac Boibli da*no* robatar sain—LL.].
,, l. 25, *after* Samaisce *insert* Now those belonged to Boible.
,, l. 37, *for* hardly . . . Ulster *read* in Kerry; see the *Four Masters*, ed. O'Donovan, i, p. 86.
P. 487, l. 2, *muccada* should perhaps be corrected into múchtha, "of smothering". The contest was, apparently, to see which of the two combatants could drown the other. Compare *Rev. Celt.*, v, 200.
P. 488, l. 17, *after* toeb *insert* Síde.
,, l. 35, *before* Nenta *insert* Síd.
P. 489, l. 13, *add* Síd Nenta was a fairy mansion in Connaught, O'Curry, *Lectures*, 286, 591.
,, l. 22, *for* aib *read* aibda.
P. 491, l. 16, *add* Perhaps the latter is Magh Mossaidh, which O'Curry (*Lectures*, pp. 485, 486) says is part of the barony of Eliogarty, not far from Cashel.
P. 495, ll. 3, 4, *read* They, both hounds and men, drove the swine before them.
,, ll. 28, 32, *for* hounds *read* wolves.
,, l. 42, *for* hounds *read* wolves.
P. 502, l. 16, *for* Duiublind *read* Duiublind.
P. 505, l. 11, *read* thabairt dochum.
,, l. 19, *for* cre[d]umai *for*sin curuch *read* (with the corrector of LL.) forsin curuch credumai, "on the boat of bronze".
P. 509, l. 20, *for* then *read* there.
P. 510, l. 10, *for* doaing *read* do[d]aing.
P. 516, col. 2, *insert* Mag Luirg, 30.

The Edinburgh Dinnshenchas.

INDEX OF PLACES.

Achad Abla, 71
Ard Fothaid, 60
Ard Ladrann, 57
Ard Macha, 61
Belach dá Liacc, 55
Benn Bairchi, 69
Benn Boguine, 53
Benn Codail, 72
Benn Etair, 77
Benn Foibni, 59
Brí Léith, 61
Carn Corrshlébe, 75
Carrac Cé, 75
Céis Corainn, 54
Cera, 67
Cnámchoill, 73
Cnucha, 77
Coire mBreccain, 58
Corrshlíab, 75
Cruach Aigle, 67
Cruachu, 56
Cualnge, 61, 63

Cúil Cesra, 57
Druim Bethaig, 76
Druim Clasaig, 76
Druim Fingin, 76
Dún na mBarc, 57
Dún Sobairchi, 69
Emain, 61, 64
Fert Finntain, 57
Findloch Cera, 67
Forcarthu, 73
Inber Cichmaini, 74
Inis Fuata, 77
Lia Lindgadain, 65
Loch Cé, 75
Loch Cuan, 69
Loch da Caech, 69
Loch n-Echach, 55
Loch n-Eirne, 56
Loch Ríb, 55
Loch Ruide, 69
Lusmag, 71
Mag nAilbi, 66

Mag nAirne, 75
Mag Coba, 62
Mag Corainn, 54
Mag Cúma, 73
Mag nDairbthenn, 55
Mag nDoirbe, 73
Mag nDumach, 76
Mag Find, 55
Mag Lamraide, 57
Mag Muaich, 73
Mag Mugna, 66
Mag Tailten, 68
Mag Tuired, 75
Sliab Betha, 57
Sliab Callainn, 63
Sliab Fuait, 64, 77
Tailtiu, 68
Telach Bela, 70
Tendais, 76
Tlachtga, 73
Tráig Tuirbi, 70
Tul Tuinne, 57

WHITLEY STOKES.

Made in the USA
Middletown, DE
04 January 2023

21392130R00021